CHICKEN

CHICKEN

VERSATILE, HEALTHY AND DELICIOUS
DISHES TO CREATE

REBO
PRODUCTIONS

Contents

Introduction

Chicken is one of the most versatile meats available, and probably the most popular. You can choose from a whole range of different cuts – drumsticks, breasts, wings and whole birds – and each can be cooked by a variety of methods.

Chicken marries well with all kinds of herbs, spices and seasonings. It takes mild, creamy flavours equally well as robust and fiery ones, enabling you to cater for all kinds of tastes. When you are short of time, simple yet tasty chicken dishes can be prepared and cooked in a matter of minutes. Alternatively, you can dress up chicken and create a much more elaborate meal for entertaining.

When it comes to health considerations, chicken is a winner. It is low in fat and contains a high proportion of unsaturated fatty acids, which is an important factor in low-cholesterol diets. Remove the skin from chicken and use only the white meat, and chicken rates even lower in the fat and calories stakes. It also has a high-protein value, and contains useful amounts of thiamine, riboflavin and nicotinic acid from the Vitamin B complex.

Always buy top-quality chicken, for maximum flavour and nutrients. Look for organic and free-range chicken, and choose corn-fed chickens for special-occasion dishes.

Here is a selection of exciting and varied chicken dishes for you to create and enjoy. Some are quick and easy recipes for everyday eating, others are luxury dishes for special occasions. We have also included a range of 'lean & light' dishes, for those watching their calorie and fat intakes, as well as hot and spicy options to pep up your culinary repertoire. Choose from the ever-popular classic chicken dishes of the great international cuisines to creative and contemporary recipes, to delight the adventurous!

Chicken Soup with Red Lentils

A hearty soup of Turkish origin, invitingly topped with grated cheese and crispy croutons.

Preparation time: 15 minutes • Cooking time: 1 hour • Serves: 4

Ingredients

2 skinless, boneless chicken breasts	700 ml (1¼ pints) chicken stock
90 ml (6 tbsp) olive oil	A sprig of fresh thyme
1 clove garlic, finely chopped	1 bay leaf
1 onion, finely chopped	Juice of 1 lemon
1 red pepper, seeded and sliced	5 ml (1 tsp) paprika
1 chilli, seeded and thinly sliced	Salt and freshly ground pepper
350 ml (12 oz) red lentils	4 slices white bread
30-45 ml (2-3 tbsp) plain flour	100 g (3½ oz) grated Cheddar or Gruyère cheese

Method

1
Cut the chicken fillets into small cubes. Heat 60 ml (4 tbsp) of the olive oil in a saucepan, add the chicken pieces and cook until browned all over, stirring occasionally.

2
Add the garlic, onion, red pepper and chilli, stir to mix, then cook for 5 minutes, stirring occasionally.

3
Rinse the lentils under cold running water and drain well before adding to the chicken.
Stir the flour into the cooking juices, then add the chicken stock.

4
Bring the soup to the boil, then add the herbs, lemon juice, paprika, salt and pepper. Reduce to a simmer, cover and cook for 40-50 minutes, stirring occasionally, until the chicken and lentils are cooked and tender.

5
Meanwhile, brush a baking tray with the remaining olive oil and heat in an oven at 200°C/400°C/Gas Mark 6.
Cut the bread into small cubes and toss in the preheated olive oil. Cook in the oven until golden.

6
Check the seasoning of the soup and adjust as necessary. Remove and discard the thyme and bay leaf.
Ladle into warmed soup bowls and serve the soup hot, sprinkled with grated cheese and the croutons.

Serving suggestion
Serve with extra slices of fresh crusty bread.

Variations
Use turkey in place of chicken. Use 1 leek in place of the onion.

Cook's tip
Alternatively, the croutons can be fried in a frying pan, turning frequently, until golden brown all over.

Chinese Chicken Soup

A quick and easy version of an Oriental-style chicken and noodle soup.

Preparation time: 10 minutes, plus 2-3 hours soaking time • Cooking time: 1½ hours • Serves: 4-6

Ingredients

25 g (1 oz) dried Chinese mushrooms	50 g (1¾ oz) rice noodles
2 chicken stock cubes	350-g (12-oz) can bamboo shoots, drained and cut into strips
1 oven-ready chicken, weighing about 1 kg (2 lb 4 oz)	Soy sauce, to taste
150 g (5½ oz) dried soup vegetables	Sambal oelek (Asian chilli sauce), to taste

Method

1

Soak the Chinese mushrooms in a bowl of water for 2-3 hours. Drain, then slice into strips and set aside.

2

In a large saucepan, bring 2½ litres (4½ pints) water to the boil and crumble the stock cubes into the boiling water. Add the chicken and dried soup vegetables and bring to the boil. Cover, reduce the heat and simmer for about 1 hour.

3

Remove the chicken from the stock and set the stock aside. Remove the chicken flesh from the bones, discarding the bones and skin.

4

Cut the chicken meat into small pieces, place in a bowl with the rice noodles and cover with boiling water. Set aside for about 3-4 minutes, then rinse with cold water and drain.

5

Add the chicken and noodles to the stock in the pan with the Chinese mushrooms and stir to mix. Bring back to the boil, cover and cook for a further 20 minutes.

6

Add the bamboo shoots and reheat gently until hot.

7

Stir in some soy sauce and sambal oelek to taste, ladle into warmed soup bowls and serve hot.

Serving suggestion
Serve with thick slices of fresh crusty white bread.

Variations
Use a small turkey in place of the chicken. Use canned baby sweetcorn, sliced, in place of bamboo shoots.

Cook's tip
Sambal oelek is available from Oriental food stores.

Chicken and Mixed Vegetable Soup

This traditional German soup is both filling and full of flavour.

Preparation time: 20 minutes • Cooking time: 45 minutes • Serves: 4

Ingredients

45 ml (3 tbsp) olive oil	15 ml (1 tbsp) plain flour
2 skinless, boneless chicken breasts, cut into small pieces	500 ml (18 fl oz) chicken stock
	30 ml (2 tbsp) crème fraîche
2 skinless, boneless chicken thighs, cut into small pieces	1 sprig fresh chervil, chopped
2 onions, chopped	1 bunch watercress, chopped
1 clove garlic, crushed	A pinch of freshly ground nutmeg
2 leeks, thinly sliced	A pinch of sugar
2 sticks celery, finely chopped	5 ml (1 tsp) corn schnapps
2 carrots, finely chopped	Salt and freshly ground black pepper

Method

1

Heat the oil in a saucepan, add the chicken and cook until browned all over, stirring occasionally.

2

Add the onions, garlic, leeks, celery and carrots and cook for 5 minutes, stirring occasionally.
Stir in the flour, then cook for 1 minute, stirring.

3

Gradually stir in the stock, then bring to the boil. Cover, reduce the heat and simmer for about 30 minutes, until the chicken is cooked and tender, stirring occasionally.

4

Stir in the crème fraîche, chervil, watercress, nutmeg, sugar, schnapps and salt and pepper and reheat gently.
Ladle into warmed soup bowls to serve.

Serving suggestion

Serve with crisp croutons or garlic bread.

Variations

Use turkey or goose in place of chicken. Use 2 parsnips in place of the carrots.

Chicken and Mushroom Salad

This rich salad combines a variety of different mushrooms with tender strips of fried chicken,
tossed in a basil-flavoured mayonnaise dressing.

Preparation time: 15 minutes, plus cooking and chilling time • Cooking time: 10 minutes • Serves: 4

Ingredients

15 g (½ oz) dried cep mushrooms	1 egg yolk
30 ml (2 tbsp) vegetable oil	5 ml (1 tsp) mustard
250 g (9 oz) skinless, boneless chicken breast, cut into thin strips	5 ml (1 tsp) sugar
	15 ml (1 tbsp) wine vinegar or lemon juice
Salt and freshly ground black pepper	125 ml (4 fl oz) olive oil
250 g (9 oz) mushrooms or chanterelles, sliced	30 ml (2 tbsp) crème fraîche
1 bunch spring onions, chopped	45 ml (3 tbsp) chopped fresh basil

Method

1

Soak the dried cep in 125 ml (4 fl oz) lukewarm water in a bowl. Set aside for 5 minutes.

2

Heat the oil in a pan, add the chicken and fry for about 2-3 minutes, until golden brown all over and cooked.
Season with salt and pepper, remove from the pan and set aside to cool.

3

Add the sliced mushrooms or chanterelles to the pan, season, then add the cep with their soaking water. Bring to the boil,
then reduce the heat and simmer for about 5 minutes. Remove the pan from the heat and set aside to cool.

4

Place the spring onions in a salad bowl with the mushrooms and chicken and stir gently to mix.

5

To make the mayonnaise, in a bowl mix together the egg yolk, mustard, sugar and wine vinegar or lemon juice until creamy,
then gradually beat in the olive oil a little at a time until a thick mayonnaise is formed. Stir in the crème fraîche
and chopped basil and spoon over the salad. Stir gently to mix. Cover and chill for 1 hour before serving.

Serving suggestion

Serve with fresh crusty bread rolls.

Variations

Use shiitake or oyster mushrooms in place of the cultivated mushrooms or chanterelles. Use 15-30 ml (1-2 tbsp)
chopped fresh parsley or tarragon in place of the basil.

Cook's tip

If the mayonnaise mixture curdles when adding the oil, beat a second egg yolk in a separate bowl,
then add to the curdled mixture drop by drop.

Parisian Salad

An attractive salad of mixed white and black grapes, chicken breast, button mushrooms and Cheddar cheese.

Preparation time: 20 minutes • Serves: 4

Ingredients

375 g (13 oz) white and black grapes	Salt and freshly ground pepper
175 g (6 oz) button mushrooms, braised	A pinch of sugar
200 g (7 oz) Cheddar cheese	15 ml (1 tbsp) wine vinegar
250 g (9 oz) cold cooked chicken breast	125 ml (4 fl oz) olive oil
1 egg yolk	45 ml (3 tbsp) yogurt
5-10 ml (1-2 tsp) mustard	Sprigs of fresh lovage or flat-leafed parsley, to garnish

Method

1

Wash the grapes and slice them in half. Remove the seeds and discard, then place the grapes in a salad bowl. Thinly slice the mushrooms and cut the cheese into small cubes. Add to the bowl and stir gently to mix.

2

Dice the chicken breast and add to the bowl. Stir to mix and set aside.

3

To make the mayonnaise, in a bowl mix the egg yolk, mustard, salt and pepper, sugar and wine vinegar together until creamy. Gradually beat in the olive oil a little at a time until a thick mayonnaise is formed. Stir in the yogurt.

4

Add the mayonnaise to the salad and toss gently to mix. Serve immediately, garnished with fresh lovage or parsley.

Serving suggestion
Serve with warmed fresh crusty French bread.

Variations
Use canned, flaked fish, such as salmon or tuna, in place of the chicken. Use Gruyère or Red Leicester in place of the Cheddar.

Smoked Chicken Salad

The smoked flavour of the chicken is perfectly complemented by the piquancy of blue cheese
and the creaminess of avocado in this unusual yet quick and easy salad.

Preparation time: 15 minutes • Serves: 2

Ingredients

1 smoked cooked skinless, boneless chicken breast	20 g (¾ oz) blue cheese
1 ripe avocado pear	Salt and freshly ground black pepper
1 beefsteak tomato	60 ml (4 tbsp) olive oil
10 black olives	15 ml (1 tbsp) wine vinegar
1 sprig of fresh flat-leafed parsley	25 g (1 oz) cashew nuts

Method

1

Dice the chicken and place in a bowl. Peel, halve and stone the avocado and slice the flesh. Seed and dice the tomato.
Stone and slice the olives. Wash the parsley, dry and finely chop the leaves.

2

Add the avocado, olives and parsley to the chicken and gently stir together.

3

Crumble the cheese with a fork, place in a bowl and mix with the salt, pepper, oil and wine vinegar. Spoon over the salad.

4

Garnish the salad with cashew nuts and serve immediately.

Serving suggestion

Serve with oatcakes or slices of bread.

Variations

Use almonds or walnuts in place of the cashew nuts. Use an unsmoked cooked chicken breast in place of the smoked chicken.

Cook's tip

To test if an avocado pear is ripe, gently press at the stalk end. The pear is ripe if it feels slightly soft;
if too soft, the avocado will be over-ripe.

Chicken and Mango Salad

This recipe is a perfect way of turning leftover chicken into a delicious light meal.

Preparation time: 25 minutes • Serves: 4

Ingredients

30 ml (2 tbsp) chopped fresh chives or 15 ml (1 tbsp) dried chives	*5 ml (1 tsp) powdered mustard*
	Salt and freshly ground black pepper
60 ml (4 tbsp) dry white wine	*1 large mango*
105 ml (7 tbsp) mayonnaise	*450 g (1 lb) cooked skinless, boneless chicken breast*
105 ml (7 tbsp) soured cream	*Chopped fresh chives, to garnish*

Method

1

Place the chives and wine in a small pan and simmer, uncovered, for about 5 minutes, until reduced to only 15-30 ml (1-2 tbsp).

2

Pour through a fine sieve, pushing the chives to extract as much of their essence as possible. Set aside.

3

In a bowl, mix the mayonnaise with the soured cream, mustard and about 15 ml (1 tbsp) of the chive essence. Do not let the dressing become too thin, particularly if the dish is being made in advance.

4

Check the seasoning, adding salt and pepper if necessary.

5

Peel, stone and slice the mango. Cut the cold chicken into slices of approximately the same size as the mango.

6

Place the mango and cold chicken in a shallow dish, pour over the dressing and toss lightly so that all the pieces are coated. Serve immediately, garnished with chopped chives.

Serving suggestion

Serve with thick slices of fresh crusty bread.

Variations

Use avocado pear(s) in place of mango. Used cooked turkey or pork in place of chicken. Use parsley in place of the chives.

Cook's tip

If making this salad in advance, do not coat with the dressing until ready to serve.

Chicken Pilaf à la Turk

A tasty chicken and sultana rice dish.

Preparation time: 1½ hours • Cooking time: 15 minutes • Serves: 4

Ingredients

1 chicken, weighing about 1.5 kg (3 lb 5 oz)	*Salt and freshly ground black pepper*
150 g (5½ oz) mixed soup vegetables, such as carrots, turnips, leeks and swede, coarsely chopped	*Cayenne pepper, to taste*
55 g (2 oz) butter	*2.5-cm (1-in) piece root ginger, peeled and finely chopped*
100 g (3½ oz) onion, sliced	*125 g (4½ oz) sultanas*
1 red pepper, seeded and cut into chunks	*125 g (4½ oz) white rice*

Method

1
Fillet the breast of the chicken and remove the legs. Remove the bones and cut the meat into large chunks.

2
Place the bones in a saucepan with the mixed soup vegetables. Add 1 litre (1¾ pints) water and, with the pan uncovered, bring to the boil over a gentle heat. Simmer, uncovered, for about 1½ hours. Strain, reserving the stock and discarding the bones and vegetables. Set aside.

3
Melt the butter in a pan, add the chicken pieces and cook until sealed all over. Add the onion and pepper and cook until softened, stirring occasionally, then season with salt, pepper and cayenne pepper to taste.

4
Add the ginger and 125 ml (4 fl oz) of the reserved chicken stock to the chicken. Cover the pan, bring to the boil, then reduce the heat and cook for about 10 minutes, until cooked and tender, stirring occasionally. Stir in the sultanas.

5
Meanwhile, place the rice in a saucepan with 250 ml (9 fl oz) of the chicken stock and some salt. Cover, bring to the boil and cook for about 12 minutes, until cooked and tender. Drain the rice and mix the chicken mixture and rice together. Serve immediately.

Serving suggestion
Serve with a mixed leaf or chopped salad.

Variations
Use leeks in place of the onion. Use raisins or chopped ready-to-eat apricots in place of the sultanas.

Red Cabbage and Chicken Medley

A delicious combination of lightly cooked and dressed red cabbage and pan-fried chicken sprinkled with chopped walnuts.

Preparation time: 15 minutes • Cooking time: 20 minutes • Serves: 4

Ingredients

500 g (1 lb 2 oz) red cabbage	Salt and freshly ground black pepper
30 ml (2 tbsp) white wine vinegar	25 g (1 oz) butter
5 ml (1 tsp) honey	300 g (10½ oz) skinless, boneless chicken breasts
30 ml (2 tbsp) lemon juice	
15 ml (1 tbsp) red wine vinegar	10 walnut halves

Method

1

Remove the stalk and outer leaves from the cabbage and discard. Wash the cabbage and finely slice. Bring a large saucepan of salted water to the boil, stir in the wine vinegar, then add the cabbage and blanch for about 1 minute.

2

Drain well, then add the honey, lemon juice and red wine vinegar to the cabbage and mix well. Season with salt and pepper. Set aside while cooking the chicken.

3

Melt the butter in a frying pan, add the chicken and cook for 15-20 minutes, turning to brown both sides, until cooked and tender. Season with salt and pepper.

4

Arrange the cabbage mixture on 4 serving plates, slice the cooked chicken into thin strips and arrange over the cabbage. Chop the walnuts and sprinkle over the chicken to serve.

Serving suggestion

Serve with boiled new potatoes and cooked fresh vegetables such as baby carrots or courgettes.

Variations

Use duck in place of chicken. Use green or white cabbage or spinach in place of the red cabbage.

Chicken Livers with Chinese Leaves and Almonds

Stir-fries are an ideal 'lean and light' option because the ingredients are cooked quickly in the minimum amount of oil, thereby preserving all the nutrients, texture and colour of the food. Cooked in this way, chicken livers are tender and delicious.

Preparation time: 25 minutes • Cooking time: 10 minutes • Serves: 4

Ingredients

225 g (8 oz) chicken livers	*8-10 Chinese leaves, finely shredded*
30 ml (2 tbsp) vegetable oil	*10 ml (2 tsp) cornflour,*
55 g (2 oz) split blanched almonds	*mixed with 15 ml (1 tbsp) cold water*
1 clove garlic, peeled	*30 ml (2 tbsp) soy sauce*
55 g (2 oz) mangetout	*150 ml (¼ pint) chicken stock*

Method

1
Remove any discoloured areas or pieces of fat from the chicken livers. Cut the livers into evenly sized pieces.

2
Heat the oil in a wok or large frying pan over a high heat. Reduce the heat to medium and add the almonds. Cook, stirring continuously, until the almonds are golden brown. Remove with a slotted spoon and drain on absorbent kitchen paper.

3
Add the garlic to the pan, stir-fry for 1-2 minutes to flavour the oil, then remove and discard.

4
Add the chicken livers and stir-fry for 2-3 minutes. Remove the chicken livers, place on a plate and set aside.

5
Add the mangetout and stir-fry for 1 minute, then add the Chinese leaves and stir-fry for a further 1 minute. Remove the vegetables to the plate with the chicken livers and set aside.

6
In a small bowl or jug, mix the cornflour mixture with the soy sauce and stock. Add to the pan, stirring, and bring to the boil. Cook until thickened and clear.

7
Return all the other ingredients to the sauce and reheat for 30 seconds. Serve immediately.

Serving suggestion
Serve with boiled or fried rice or Chinese noodles.

Variations
Use chicken breast, cut into very thin strips, in place of chicken livers and stir-fry for about 8 minutes, or until cooked through. Use raw unsalted cashew nuts in place of almonds.

Cook's tips
Be sure to remove any discoloured portions from the livers, since these can cause a bitter taste.
Livers can be served slightly pink in the middle, if you like.

Marjoram Chicken with Vegetables

A fragrant herb and wine-flavoured chicken dish, simply baked in the oven.

Preparation time: 10 minutes • Cooking time: 1 hour • Serves: 4

Ingredients

1 oven-ready chicken, weighing about 1.5 kg (3 lb 5 oz)	*45-75 ml (3-5 tbsp) chopped fresh marjoram*
Salt and freshly ground pepper	*250 ml (9 fl oz) white wine*
2 cloves garlic	*1-2 yellow peppers, about 225 g (8 oz) in weight*
55 g (2 oz) butter, softened, for greasing	*500 g (1 lb 2 oz) beefsteak tomatoes*

Method

1

Cut the chicken into 4 pieces and rub salt and pepper into the skin. Peel the cloves of garlic and rub into the meat.
Sprinkle 30-45 ml (2-3 tbsp) marjoram into a greased ovenproof dish and add the chicken and wine.

2

Bake in a preheated oven at 220°C/425°F/Gas Mark 7 for about 40 minutes, basting the chicken once or twice with the wine.

3

Meanwhile, seed and slice the peppers into strips. Set aside. Remove the skins from the tomatoes, cut into quarters and seed.

4

Add the sliced peppers and tomatoes to the chicken and stir to mix.

5

Return to the oven and bake for a further 10-20 minutes, until the chicken and vegetables are cooked and tender.

6

Before serving, sprinkle a further 15-30 ml (1-2 tbsp) chopped marjoram over the chicken and vegetables and serve immediately.

Serving suggestion

Serve with oven-baked potatoes and cooked fresh vegetables such as cauliflower and courgettes.

Variations

Use oregano or parsley in place of marjoram. Use plum tomatoes in place of beefsteak tomatoes.

Cook's tip

Skin tomatoes by immersing them in boiling water for 15 seconds, then plunge in cold water.
Peel away the skin using a small knife.

Chicken with Lemon Julienne

Lean chicken served with a tangy julienne of fresh vegetables makes a delicious main course.

Preparation time: 35 minutes • Cooking time: 1 hour • Serves: 4-6

Ingredients

1 oven-ready chicken, weighing 1.5 kg (3 lb 5 oz)	15 ml (1 tbsp) chopped fresh basil
30 ml (2 tbsp) olive oil	1 bay leaf
30 ml (2 tbsp) soft margarine	Juice and finely grated rind of 2 small lemons
2 sticks celery, cut into matchsticks	Salt and freshly ground black pepper
2 carrots, cut into matchsticks	A pinch of sugar (optional)
1 small onion, peeled and thinly sliced	Lemon slices, to garnish

Method

1

Cut the chicken into 8 pieces with a sharp knife or a cook's cleaver. Cut the chicken lengthways down the breastbone and through the backbone to halve it completely.

2

Cut the chicken halves in half again, slitting between the leg joint diagonally up and around the breast joint.

3

Finally, cut each chicken quarter in half by cutting away the drumsticks from the leg thigh joint, and the wings from the breast joints.

4

Remove and discard the skin from the chicken joints by pulling and cutting with a sharp knife.

5

Heat the oil and margarine in a large frying pan. Add the chicken pieces and gently fry, turning frequently, to brown evenly all over.

6

Place the chicken pieces on a plate and set aside.

7

Stir the celery, carrots and onion into the chicken juices. Cook over a gently heat for about 3 minutes, or until just beginning to soften but not brown.

8

Add the basil, bay leaf, lemon juice and rind, 150 ml (¼ pint) water and salt and pepper, mix well and cook for 2-3 minutes, stirring occasionally.

9

Return the chicken portions to the casserole and bring the mixture to the boil. Cover the pan and reduce the heat. Allow the casserole to simmer for about 35-45 minutes, or until the chicken is tender and the juices run clear when the meat is pierced with a sharp knife.

10

Place the chicken and vegetables on to a warmed serving dish and discard the bay leaf.

11

Boil the sauce rapidly to thicken if necessary. Adjust the flavour of the sauce, adding the sugar if using. Spoon the sauce over the chicken, garnish with the lemon slices and serve immediately.

Serving suggestion
Serve with boiled rice and a green salad.

Variations
Use 175 g (6 oz) swede in place of the carrots. Use lime juice in place of lemon juice.

Cook's tip
Make sure that the chicken pieces are patted dry with absorbent kitchen paper before you fry them, otherwise the oil will spit.

Chicken with Stuffed Peppers

Try a different stuffing from the usual meat and rice variety for these light tasting peppers.

Preparation time: 35 minutes • Cooking time: 45 minutes • Serves: 6

Ingredients

3 large green or red peppers	*10 ml (2 tsp) chopped fresh parsley*
55 g (2 oz) butter or margarine	*Salt and freshly ground pepper*
1 small onion, finely chopped	*½ medium loaf of stale bread, made into crumbs*
1 stick celery, finely chopped	
1 clove garlic, crushed	*1-2 eggs, beaten*
3 chicken breasts, skinned, boned and diced	*55 g (2 oz) dry breadcrumbs*

Method

1

Cut the peppers in half lengthwise and remove the cores and seeds. Leave the stems attached, if you wish.

2

Melt the butter or margarine in a frying pan and add the onion, celery, garlic and chicken.
Cook over a moderate heat for about 15-20 minutes, until the vegetables are softened and the chicken
is cooked and tender. Add the parsley and season with salt and pepper.

3

Stir in the stale breadcrumbs and add enough beaten egg to make the mixture hold together.

4

Spoon some of the filling into each pepper half, mounding the top slightly. Place the peppers in
a baking dish which holds them closely together.

5

Pour enough water into the dish to come about 1 cm (½ inch) up the sides of the peppers. Cover and bake in a preheated
oven at 180°C/350°F/Gas Mark 4 for about 45 minutes, or until the peppers are just tender.

6

Sprinkle each pepper half with the dry breadcrumbs and place under a preheated grill until golden brown. Serve immediately.

Serving suggestion

Serve as a light lunch or supper with a mixed leaf salad.

Variations

Use spring onions in place of the small onion. Add chopped nuts or stoned black olives to the filling.

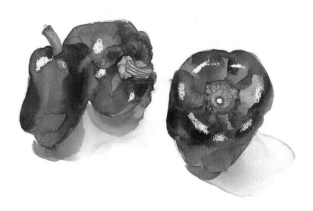

Apricot Chicken with Mint

A special chicken recipe with a light, yogurt-based sauce of a pale apricot colour and a delightfully fresh flavour. It can be served hot or cold.

Preparation time: 20 minutes, plus marinating time • Cooking time: 45 minutes • Serves: 4

Ingredients

8 chicken thighs or drumsticks, skinned	*30 ml (2 tbsp) chopped fresh mint or 10 ml (2 tsp) dried mint*
55 g (2 oz) onion, finely chopped	
1 orange	*150 ml (¼ pint) dry white wine*
30 ml (2 tbsp) lemon juice	*Salt and freshly ground black pepper*
55 g (2 oz) ready-to-eat dried apricots	*45-60 ml (3-4 tbsp) thick natural yogurt, to serve*

Method

1

Place the chicken in a flameproof casserole dish and add the onion, finely grated rind of the orange with 60 ml (4 tbsp) of the juice and all the remaining ingredients except the yogurt. Mix well. Be generous with the mint, since much of the flavour cooks away.

2

Cover and marinate for 2-4 hours or overnight in the refrigerator.

3

Allow the chicken to come to room temperature, then bake, covered, in a preheated oven at 190°C/375°F/Gas Mark 5 for 45 minutes, or until cooked and tender. Remove the chicken and keep hot.

4

Purée the remaining casserole in a food processor or liquidiser, then push through a sieve, using the back of a soup ladle, into a saucepan.

5

Reheat but do not allow to boil. Remove from the heat and stir in the yogurt, tasting all the time to get a pouring sauce that is rich but light in flavour. Adjust the seasoning with salt and pepper, then pour the sauce over the chicken and serve immediately.

Serving suggestion
You can serve the dish hot, with the sauce in a separate container as a dip.
Serve with a mixed green salad and fresh crusty French bread.

Variations
Use red wine or apple juice in place of the white wine. Use dried pears or peaches in place of apricots.

Herby Lemon Chicken

Chicken drumsticks crisply coated in a flavourful crumb and served with a fresh-tasting herb and lemon butter.

Preparation time: 20 minutes • Cooking time: 30-40 minutes • Serves: 4

Ingredients

175 g (6 oz) fresh white breadcrumbs	Plain flour, for dusting
30 ml (2 tbsp) chopped fresh parsley	1 egg, beaten
30 ml (2 tbsp) chopped fresh tarragon	
	For the lemon and herb butter
Finely grated rind of 1 lemon	115 g (4 oz) slightly salted butter
Salt and freshly ground black pepper	Finely grated rind of 1 lemon
15 ml (1 tbsp) Dijon mustard	A squeeze of lemon juice
55 g (2 oz) butter	30 ml (2 tbsp) chopped fresh parsley
8 chicken drumsticks, skinned	30 ml (2 tbsp) chopped fresh tarragon

Method

1
Place the breadcrumbs in a large shallow bowl and add the parsley, tarragon and lemon rind.
Season with salt and pepper and mix well.

2
Place the mustard and butter in a saucepan and heat until melted. Remove from the heat and add the breadcrumb mixture, stirring well to coat all the breadcrumbs in butter. Set aside to cool.

3
Coat each chicken drumstick, one at a time, with flour. Dip, one at a time, in the beaten egg, then roll in the breadcrumbs, gently pressing on the mixture to give an even coating.

4
Lay the drumsticks on a rack over a roasting tin and bake in a preheated oven at 200°C/400°F/Gas Mark 6 for 30-40 minutes, or until golden brown and crisp.

5
Meanwhile, thoroughly mix together all the lemon and herb butter ingredients. Place on a piece of greaseproof paper and pat into a cylinder shape using a knife. Roll up the butter inside the paper and twist the ends to seal. Chill until firm. To serve, unwrap and slice into rounds to accompany the chicken.

6
Serve the hot chicken drumsticks with the lemon and herb butter alongside.

Serving suggestion
Serve with oven-baked potatoes and a green salad.

Variation
Use whole-grain mustard in place of Dijon mustard.

Chicken Cacciatore

The use of herbs, wine and vinegar gives a wonderful hearty flavour to this delectable classic Italian dish.

Preparation time: 15 minutes • Cooking time: 1 hour 15 minutes • Serves: 4-6

Ingredients

60 ml (4 tbsp) olive oil	*15 ml (1 tbsp) chopped fresh parsley*
1.5 kg (3 lb 5 oz) chicken pieces	*10 ml (2 tsp) chopped fresh oregano*
2 onions, sliced	*10 ml (2 tsp) chopped fresh basil*
3 cloves garlic, crushed	*1 bay leaf*
225 g (8 oz) button mushrooms, quartered	*450 g (1 lb) canned tomatoes*
	150 ml (¼ pint) chicken stock
150 ml (¼ pint) red wine	*Freshly ground black pepper*
15 ml (1 tbsp) red wine vinegar	*A pinch of sugar*

Method

1
Heat the oil in a large frying pan and lay the chicken pieces, skin side down, in one layer.

2
Cook for 3-4 minutes, then turn each piece over. Continue cooking and turning the chicken portions until well browned all over. Place the chicken portions on a plate, set aside and keep hot.

3
Add the onions and garlic to the oil and chicken juices in the frying pan. Cook gently for 2-3 minutes, or until they are just beginning to brown.

4
Add the mushrooms to the pan and cook for about 1 minute, stirring continuously. Pour the wine and wine vinegar into the pan and boil rapidly to reduce to about half the original quantity.

5
Add the fresh herbs, bay leaf and tomatoes, stirring well to break up the tomatoes. Stir in the stock and season with pepper and sugar.

6
Return the chicken to the tomato sauce, stir to mix, then cover with a tight-fitting lid.
Simmer for about 1 hour, or until the chicken is cooked and tender. Serve immediately.

Serving suggestion
Serve with boiled rice or pasta and a mixed salad.

Variations
Use the delicious sauce in this recipe with any other meat of choice, such as pork or turkey.
Use sliced fresh wild mushrooms in place of button mushrooms.

Cook's tip
Remove and discard the skin from the chicken to reduce fat and calories.

Hot Chicken with Peaches

Tangy with fresh ginger and fruit vinegar, this unusual chicken dish is ideal for a summer supper.

Preparation time: 25 minutes, plus marinating time • Cooking time: 15 minutes • Serves: 2

Ingredients

350 g (12 oz) skinless, boneless chicken meat	30 ml (2 tbsp) olive oil
30 ml (2 tbsp) fruit vinegar (or cider vinegar)	30 ml (2 tbsp) dry white wine
	Salt and freshly ground black pepper
15 ml (1 tbsp) finely grated root ginger	15 ml (1 tbsp) sliced fresh mint
350-450 g (12 oz-1 lb) fresh peaches	Fresh mint sprigs, to garnish

Method

1

If using chicken breast meat, cut into 3 or 4 long, thin strips. If using thigh or drumstick meat, keep in large pieces.

2

Place the chicken in a shallow dish with the fruit or cider vinegar and the grated ginger.
Stir to mix, then cover and leave to marinate in a cool place for at least 2 hours.

3

Meanwhile, drop the peaches into boiling water for 2 minutes, then peel, stone and cut into segments.

4

Drain the marinade from the chicken and reserve. Heat the oil in a large frying pan, then add the chicken
and cook over a medium heat for 5-7 minutes, turning occasionally, until cooked and tender.

5

Place the chicken on a warm dish and keep hot. Pour the marinade and the wine into the pan, season and,
when hot, slide in the peaches and heat through without stirring.

6

Sprinkle the sliced mint leaves into the hot liquid, and the moment they have wilted, remove the pan from the heat.
Serve the chicken topped with the peaches and with the hot vinaigrette strained over the top.
Serve immediately, garnished with fresh mint sprigs.

Serving suggestion

Serve on top of a mixed salad, or accompanied by a selection of plainly cooked, seasonal fresh
vegetables such as carrots and courgettes.

Variations

If you like a more savoury flavour, soften 25 g (1 oz) very finely chopped onion and/or a little garlic in the oil before
adding the chicken, but do not let either burn. Use apricots or nectarines in place of peaches.

Cook's tip

Use canned peaches if fresh are not available.

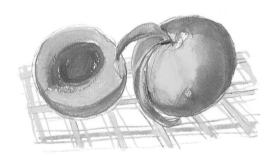

Breast of Chicken Stuffed with Roquefort

Succulent chicken breasts stuffed with a tasty blue cheese filling and deep-fried until golden and crispy.

Preparation time: 20 minutes • Cooking time: 10-15 minutes • Serves: 4

Ingredients

4 skinless, boneless chicken breasts	*85 ml (3 fl oz) Armagnac*
Salt and freshly ground black pepper	*About 25 g (1 oz) plain flour*
125 g (4½ oz) Roquefort cheese	*1 egg, lightly beaten*
40 g (1½ oz) butter, softened	*About 115 g (4 oz) breadcrumbs*
	Vegetable oil, for deep-frying

Method

1
Flatten the chicken breasts with a meat mallet or rolling pin and season with salt and pepper.

2
Crumble the cheese into a bowl, add the butter and Armagnac and mix well. Spread the mixture over the chicken breasts.

3
Fold over the chicken breasts and press the edges together. Coat first with flour, then dip in the egg
and turn over in the breadcrumbs, to coat all over.

4
Heat the oil in a deep fat fryer to 160°C/325°F. Place the chicken in a frying basket and lower into the hot oil.
Fry for 10-15 minutes, until the chicken is cooked, browned and crisp.

5
Remove from the oil, drain on absorbent kitchen paper and serve hot.

Serving suggestion
Serve with cooked fresh vegetables, such as new potatoes, mangetout and carrots.

Variations
Use another blue cheese, such as Stilton, in place of the Roquefort. Use wholemeal breadcrumbs in place of white breadcrumbs.

Chicken with Lemon Balm

A delicious combination of pan-fried chicken and a creamy, delicately herb-flavoured sauce – perfect for a quick and satisfying lunch or supper dish.

Preparation time: 15 minutes • Cooking time: 15 minutes • Serves: 4

Ingredients

4 skinless, boneless chicken breasts	*45 ml (3 tbsp) vermouth*
Salt and freshly ground pepper	*250 ml (9 fl oz) single cream*
100 g (3½ oz) butter	*20 lemon balm leaves, finely chopped*
1 shallot, finely chopped	*Fresh herb sprigs, to garnish*
400 g (14 oz) mushrooms, sliced	

Method

1

Cut the chicken breasts into thin strips and season with salt and pepper. Melt half the butter in a frying pan, add the chicken and cook for 5 minutes, stirring frequently, until cooked and tender. Remove from the pan, place on a plate and keep hot.

2

Melt the remaining butter in the cooking juices, add the shallot and mushrooms and cook for 5-10 minutes, stirring occasionally, until softened.

3

Stir in the vermouth, cream and lemon balm. Return the chicken to the sauce and heat gently, but do not allow mixture to boil.

4

Adjust the seasoning and serve immediately, garnished with fresh herb sprigs.

Serving suggestion
Serve with boiled spaghetti or tagliatelle.

Variations
Use crème fraîche in place of cream. Use fresh mixed wild mushrooms in place of standard mushrooms.
Use fresh basil in place of lemon balm.

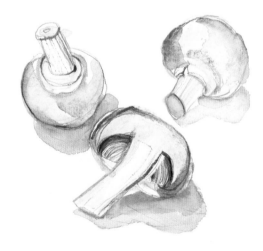

Tarragon Chicken Pancakes

These attractive pancakes look sophisticated enough for a dinner party, but are also so easy to make, you can indulge yourself at any time.

Preparation time: 20 minutes • Cooking time: 20 minutes • Serves: 4

Ingredients

115 g (4 oz) plain wholemeal flour	*225 g (8 oz) skinless, boneless chicken, chopped*
1 egg	*1 avocado pear, peeled, halved,*
600 ml (1 pint) milk	*stoned and chopped*
Vegetable oil, for frying	*10 ml (2 tsp) lemon juice*
40 g (1½ oz) plain white flour	*15 ml (1 tbsp) chopped fresh tarragon*
Salt and freshly ground pepper, to taste	*Fresh watercress sprigs, to garnish*

Method

1
Place the wholemeal flour in a large bowl and make a slight well in the centre. Break the egg into the well and begin to beat the egg carefully into the flour, incorporating only a little flour at a time.

2
Gradually add 300 ml (½ pint) of the milk to the egg and flour mixture, beating well between additions, until all the milk is incorporated and the batter is smooth.

3
Heat a little oil in a small frying pan or crêpe pan and cook about 30 ml (2 tbsp) of the batter at a time, tipping and rotating the pan so that the batter spreads evenly over the base to form a pancake. Flip the pancake over, to cook the other side.

4
Repeat this process until all the batter has been used up. Keep the pancakes warm until required.

5
Blend the white flour with a little of the remaining milk, then gradually add the rest of the milk until it is all incorporated.

6
Pour the flour and milk mixture into a small pan and cook over a moderate heat, stirring continuously, until the sauce has thickened. Season to taste. Stir in the chicken, avocado, lemon juice and tarragon.

7
Fold each hot pancake in half, then in half again, to form a triangle.

8
Carefully open part of the triangle out to form an envelope, and fill this with the chicken and avocado mixture.

9
Repeat with the remaining pancakes and filling, and serve immediately, garnished with fresh watercress sprigs.

Serving suggestion
Serving piping hot with a crisp green salad.

Variations
Use 1 mango in place of the avocado. Use parsley in place of tarragon.

Mango Chicken Thighs or Drumsticks with Coconut

This dish is slightly piquant and immensely satisfying and simple to make. It is ideal to serve cold for a picnic.

Preparation time: 15 minutes • Cooking time: 30 minutes • Serves: 4

Ingredients

8 chicken thighs or drumsticks	*5 ml (1 tsp) mild curry paste*
175 g (6 oz) mango chutney	*Lemon juice*
25 g (1 oz) desiccated coconut	*Mixed salad, to garnish*

Method

1
Skin the chicken pieces and, with a sharp knife, make a 2.5-cm (1-in) slit along the bone.

2
Cut the flesh each side of the bone to make two small pockets, but do not cut all the way through.

3
Place the mango chutney in a sieve standing over a bowl and separate the solids from the sauce.

4
Chop the mango flesh roughly, mix with the coconut and curry paste and add a squeeze of lemon juice.

5
Stuff the pockets with this mixture and place the chicken pieces in a lightly oiled or greased baking dish.

6
Stir a squeeze of lemon juice into the reserved sauce from the mango chutney,
and brush half of this over the drumsticks or thighs.

7
Bake, uncovered, in a preheated oven at 200 °C/400°F/Gas Mark 6 for 15 minutes, then brush with the remaining sauce and
return to the oven for a further 15 minutes, or until cooked through and tender. Serve hot or cold, garnished with a mixed salad.

Serving suggestion
Serve with a mixed rice and vegetable salad.

Variations
This recipe can be varied by using peach chutney or any other chutney that has large, solid pieces of fruit in it.
Use medium or strong curry paste, to suit your taste, if preferred.

Capon Breast with Bramble Sauce

An elegant yet easy-to-create dish of roasted capon breast fillets served with a rich blackberry sauce.

Preparation time: 10 minutes • Cooking time: 25 minutes • Serves: 4

Ingredients

4 fillets of capon breast, each weighing about 125-150 g (4¹/₂-5¹/₂ oz)	*150 ml (¹/₄ pint) red wine*
Salt and freshly ground black pepper	*90 ml (6 tbsp) crème fraîche*
40 g (1¹/₂ oz) butter, melted	*20 ml (³/₄ fl oz) Crème de Cassis*
400 g (14 oz) blackberries	*Fresh herb sprigs, to garnish*

Method

1

Wash the capon fillets under cold running water and pat dry with absorbent kitchen paper.
Season with salt and pepper and brush all over with the melted butter.

2

Place in a roasting tin and bake in a preheated oven at 200°C/400°F/Gas Mark 6 for about 20 minutes,
until cooked and tender. Place on a plate and keep hot. Reserve the cooking juices and pour into a saucepan.

3

Clean and wash the blackberries, then add to the cooking juices from the capon with the wine and crème fraîche.
Heat briefly, then stir in the Crème de Cassis and adjust the seasoning to taste.

4

Serve the capon fillets sliced, with the bramble sauce spooned over or alongside. Garnish with fresh herb sprigs.

Serving suggestion

Serve with duchesse potatoes and cooked fresh green beans and baby courgettes.

Variations

Use small turkey breast steaks in place of the capon. Use raspberries in place of blackberries. Use white wine in place of red wine.

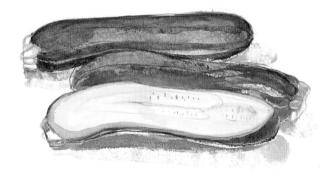

Chicken Kebabs

Prepare these kebabs up to a day in advance, then cook them in just 10 minutes for a delicious supper.

Preparation time: 15 minutes, plus 7 hours marinating time • Cooking time: 10 minutes • Serves: 4

Ingredients

1 kg (2 lb 4 oz) skinless, boneless chicken	*60 ml (4 tbsp) soy sauce*
2 onions	*30 ml (2 tbsp) lemon juice*
2 cloves garlic	*10 ml (2 tsp) ground coriander*
90 ml (6 tbsp) melted butter	*Salt and freshly ground black pepper*
	Fresh herb sprigs, to garnish

Method

1

Cut the chicken into small bite-sized pieces and set aside. Peel and thinly slice the onions and garlic and place in a shallow non-metallic dish. Add the melted butter, soy sauce, lemon juice, coriander, salt and pepper and mix well.

2

Add the chicken and stir until coated all over. Cover and refrigerate for 7 hours to marinate.

3

Remove the chicken from the marinade and pat dry with absorbent kitchen paper. Thread the chicken onto skewers and cook under a preheated grill or over hot charcoal coals for about 10 minutes, until cooked and tender. Baste frequently with the marinade to prevent the kebabs from drying out. Serve hot or cold, garnished with fresh herb sprigs.

Serving suggestion

Serve with boiled rice and a mixed pepper, tomato and onion salad.

Variations

Use pork, lamb or turkey in place of chicken. Use ground cumin in place of coriander.

Cook's tip

For a healthier option, choose reduced-sodium soy sauce.

Chicken with Chives

This superior dish of pan-fried chicken breasts stuffed with smoked salmon and served
with a creamy chive sauce is surprisingly easy to make.

Preparation time: 15 minutes • Cooking time: 20-25 minutes • Serves: 4

Ingredients

4 skinless, boneless chicken breasts, each weighing 125-150 g (4½-5½ oz)	20 g (¾ oz) melted butter
	2 shallots, finely chopped
125 g (4½ oz) smoked salmon	50 ml (2 fl oz) white wine
Salt and freshly ground pepper	100 ml (3½ fl oz) chicken stock
50 g (1¾ oz) butter, plus 50 g (1¾ oz) butter pats	250 ml (9 fl oz) double or single cream
	2 bunches of fresh chives

Method

1

Flatten the chicken breasts slightly with a cleaver, meat hammer or rolling pin and cut an opening in each breast.
Slice the smoked salmon into 4 large pieces and press 1 piece into the opening in each chicken breast.
Secure with a cocktail stick, then rub salt and pepper into the meat.

2

Melt 50 g (1¾) of the butter, add the chicken pieces and cook for about 15-20 minutes, turning occasionally,
until cooked and tender. Remove and discard the cocktail sticks. Place the chicken on a warm plate, cover and keep hot.

3

Add the melted butter to the pan, then add the shallots and cook for 5 minutes, stirring occasionally. Add the wine
and stock, bring to the boil, then reduce the heat and simmer for 5 minutes before adding the cream.

4

While the sauce is simmering, rinse and dry the chives, finely chop and stir into the sauce.
Gradually drop the butter pats into the sauce and beat in. Taste and adjust the seasoning.

5

Serve the hot cooked chicken with the chive sauce poured over.

Serving suggestion

Serve with cooked fresh vegetables such as sautéed potatoes and broccoli and cauliflower florets.

Variations

Use 1 small onion in place of the shallots. Use chopped fresh parsley or basil in place of the chives.

Cook's tip

A quick and easy way to chop fresh chives is to snip them into pieces using a pair of clean kitchen scissors.

Chicken in Lime Sauce

Almond-crusted chicken breasts served with a refreshing lime-flavoured sauce.

Preparation time: 15 minutes • Cooking time: 15-20 minutes • Serves: 4-6

Ingredients

600 g (1 lb 5 oz) skinless, boneless chicken breasts	2 limes
Salt and freshly ground black pepper	400 g (14 oz) crème fraîche
A little flour	30 ml (2 tbsp) lemon balm, finely chopped
1 egg, lightly beaten	30 ml (2 tbsp) dry vermouth
125 g (4½ oz) flaked almonds	1 lettuce, shredded
40 g (1½ oz) clarified butter	30 ml (2 tbsp) ground green peppercorns
	Lemon balm leaves, to garnish

Method

1
Season the chicken breasts with salt and pepper. Turn over in the flour, then coat with beaten egg and roll in the flaked almonds.

2
Melt the clarified butter in a frying pan, add the chicken and cook for 15-20 minutes, or until lightly browned all over, cooked and tender, turning occasionally.

3
Remove from the pan, place on a plate and set aside to cool.

4
Grate a little of the zest from the limes, cut the limes in half and squeeze out the juice. In a bowl, mix together 60 ml (4 tbsp) of the lime juice with the lime zest, crème fraîche, lemon balm and vermouth, adding salt to taste.

5
Arrange the lettuce on a serving plate and lay the chicken on top. Spoon half the sauce over the chicken, sprinkle with ground green peppercorns, garnish with lemon balm leaves and serve. Serve the remainder of the sauce separately alongside.

Serving suggestion
Serve with thick slices of fresh bread or toast.

Variations
Use chopped fresh basil or mint in place of the lemon balm. Use lemons in place of limes.

Chicken with Chargrilled Peppers and Coriander

Chargrilling peppers is a technique for removing the skins that also imparts a delicious smoky flavour to this popular vegetable.

Preparation time: 25 minutes • Cooking time: 1½ hours • Serves: 4

Ingredients

2 red peppers, halved and seeded	450 g (1 lb) canned tomatoes, drained and chopped
1 green pepper, halved and seeded	45 ml (3 tbsp) chopped fresh coriander
60 ml (4 tbsp) vegetable oil, for brushing	45 ml (3 tbsp) chopped fresh parsley
15 ml (1 tbsp) olive oil	Salt
10 ml (2 tsp) paprika	4 large skinless, boneless chicken breasts
10 ml (2 tsp) ground cumin	1 large onion, sliced
A good pinch of cayenne pepper	55 g (2 oz) flaked almonds
2 cloves garlic, crushed	Fresh herb sprigs, to garnish

Method

1

Place the peppers, cut side down, on a flat surface and gently press with the palm of your hand to flatten out.

2

Brush the skin side with 30 ml (2 tbsp) of the vegetable oil and cook under a preheated hot grill until the skin chars and splits.

3

Wrap the peppers in a clean towel for 10 minutes to cool. Unwrap the peppers and carefully peel off the charred skin. Chop the pepper flesh into thin strips and set aside.

4

Heat the olive oil in a frying pan, add the paprika, cumin, cayenne pepper and garlic and gently fry for 2 minutes, stirring to prevent the garlic from browning.

5

Stir in the tomatoes, fresh coriander and parsley and season with a little salt. Bring to the boil, then reduce the heat and simmer for 15-20 minutes, or until thick, stirring occasionally. Set aside.

6

Heat the remaining vegetable oil in a flameproof casserole dish, and fry the chicken breasts, turning frequently until they are golden brown on both sides.

7

Remove the chicken, place on a plate and set aside. Gently fry the onions in the oil for about 5 minutes, or until softened but not overcooked.

8

Return the chicken to the casserole with the onions and add about 300 ml (½ pint) water. Bring to the boil, then cover the casserole, reduce the heat and simmer for about 30 minutes, turning the chicken occasionally to prevent it from burning.

9

Remove the chicken from the casserole and place on a plate. Boil the remaining liquid rapidly to reduce to about 85 ml (3 fl oz) of stock.

10

Add the peppers and the tomato sauce to the chicken stock and stir well. Return the chicken to the casserole, cover, bring to the boil, then reduce the heat and simmer very gently for a further 30 minutes, or until the chicken is cooked and tender, stirring occasionally.

11

Arrange the chicken on a serving dish with a little of the sauce spooned over. Sprinkle with the flaked almonds and serve any remaining sauce separately. Serve immediately garnished with fresh herb sprigs.

Serving suggestion

Serve with cooked vegetables such as Brussels sprouts and cauliflower.

Saffron Chicken

The delicate colour of saffron and hot taste of chilli enliven the chicken to make this robust dish.

Preparation time: 25 minutes • Cooking time: 45 minutes • Serves: 4

Ingredients

1 oven-ready chicken, weighing about 1.5 kg (3 lb 5 oz)	*8 tomatoes, skinned, seeded and finely chopped*
30 ml (2 tbsp) olive oil	*280 g (10 oz) long-grain rice*
Salt and freshly ground black pepper	*A large pinch of saffron strands or*
1 small onion, finely chopped	*1.25 ml (¼ tsp) ground saffron*
1 clove garlic, crushed	*175 g (6 oz) frozen peas*
5-10 ml (1-2 tsp) hot chilli powder	*30 ml (2 tbsp) chopped fresh parsley*

Method

1

Cut the chicken into 8 pieces with a sharp knife or cleaver, cutting lengthways down the breast bone
and through the backbone, to halve it completely.

2

Cut the chicken halves in half again, slitting between the leg joint diagonally up and around the breast joint.

3

Cut each chicken quarter in half by cutting away the drumsticks from the leg thigh joint, and the wings from the breast joints.

4

Remove and discard the skin from the chicken joints by pulling and cutting with a sharp knife.

5

Heat the oil in a large flameproof casserole dish and fry the chicken, turning it frequently to brown evenly.
Season with a little salt and pepper, then remove from the pan, place on a plate and set aside.

6

Add the onion and garlic to the juices in the casserole dish and cook slowly until softened but not coloured, stirring occasionally.
Add the chilli powder to the onion and garlic and fry quickly for about 30 seconds, stirring.

7

Add the tomatoes and cook for about 5-10 minutes to draw off the liquid from the tomatoes, stirring occasionally.
The sauce mixture should be of a dropping consistency when this has been done.

8

Stir the rice, 700 ml (1¼ pints) boiling water and saffron into the tomato purée with the browned chicken portions. Bring
to the boil, reduce the heat, then cover the casserole dish tightly and simmer for about 20 minutes, stirring frequently.

9

Add the peas and parsley, stir well and continue to cook for a further 5-10 minutes, or until the rice is tender
and all the liquids have been absorbed, stirring once or twice. Serve immediately.

Serving suggestion

Serve with a mixed leaf salad or cooked fresh vegetables.

Variations

Use baby broad beans in place of peas. Use fresh coriander in place of parsley.

Chicken with Red Peppers

A Mediterranean-inspired dish which is wonderfully colourful and lively in flavour.

Preparation time: 35-40 minutes • Cooking: 35 minutes • Serves: 4

Ingredients

4 large red peppers	*2 cloves garlic, finely chopped*
4 skinned and boned chicken breasts	*45 ml (3 tbsp) white wine vinegar*
30 ml (2 tbsp) olive oil	*2 spring onions, finely chopped*
Salt and freshly ground pepper	*Fresh sage leaves, to garnish*
5 ml (1 tsp) paprika	

Method

1
Cut the peppers in half lengthwise and remove and discard the stems, cores and seeds.
Flatten the peppers with the palm of your hand and brush the skin sides lightly with oil.

2
Place the peppers skin side up on the rack of a preheated grill and cook about 5 cm (2 in) away from
the heat source until the skins are well blistered and charred.

3
Wrap the peppers in a clean tea-towel and set aside to cool. Peel off the skins with a small
vegetable knife and discard. Cut the peppers into thin strips and set aside.

4
Place the chicken breasts between two sheets of dampened greaseproof paper and flatten
by hitting with a rolling pin or meat mallet.

5
Heat the oil in a large frying pan. Season the chicken breasts on both sides with salt and pepper
and rub paprika into the flesh. Place in the hot oil and cook for about 15 minutes, turning frequently,
until cooked, tender and lightly browned. Remove the chicken and keep it warm.

6
Add the pepper strips, garlic, wine vinegar and spring onions to the pan and cook briefly until the vinegar loses its strong aroma.

7
Place the chicken breasts on serving plates and spoon over the pan juices.

8
Arrange the pepper mixture with the chicken and garnish with sage leaves.

Serving suggestion
Serve with sautéed potatoes and courgettes.

Variations
Used canned pimentos in place of red peppers. These will be softer, so cook the garlic, vinegar and onions until soft
before adding the pimentos. Use fresh coriander or flat-leaved parsley in place of the sage.

Tandoori Chicken

A classic Indian-style chicken dish, which is always a popular choice.

Preparation time: 20 minutes, plus marinating time • Cooking time: 20-30 minutes • Serves: 2-4

Ingredients

4 chicken legs	30 ml (2 tbsp) yogurt
7.5 ml (1½ tsp) salt	5 ml (1 tsp) sunflower or corn oil
15 ml (3 tsp) lemon juice	5 ml (1 tsp) cider vinegar
4 cloves garlic, finely chopped	5 ml (1 tsp) tomato purée
2.5-cm (1-inch) piece root ginger, peeled and finely grated	2.5 ml (½ tsp) hot chilli powder
	5 ml (1 tsp) garam masala
5 ml (1 tsp) ground coriander	15 ml (1 tbsp) lime juice
5 ml (1 tsp) caraway seeds	40 g (1½ oz) butter
5 ml (1 tsp) curry powder	Fresh herb sprigs and lemon slices, to garnish

Method

1
Wash and dry the chicken legs, then make incisions through the skin with a sharp knife. Rub 5 ml (1 tsp) of the salt into the meat and sprinkle with 10 ml (2 tsp) of the lemon juice. Set aside for 30 minutes to be absorbed.

2
Place the garlic and ginger in a bowl, add the coriander, caraway seeds, remaining lemon juice and curry powder and mix well. Add the yogurt, oil, vinegar, tomato purée, remaining salt and chilli powder and mix well.

3
Cover the chicken legs all over with this mixture, then place in a non-metallic dish, cover and leave to marinate in the refrigerator overnight.

4
Remove the chicken from the marinade and place on a grill rack in a grill pan. Grill under a preheated grill for about 20-30 minutes, turning to cook both sides, until cooked and tender.

5
Mix the garam masala with the lime juice and coat each chicken leg with this mixture. Place a knob of butter on each leg and serve immediately, garnished with fresh herb sprigs and lemon slices.

Serving suggestion
Serve with pilau rice or Indian bread.

Variations
Use the tandoori mixture to coat other pieces or joints of meat, such as pork, lamb or beef steaks.
Use red wine vinegar in place of cider vinegar.

Cook's tip
To save a little time and effort, use ready-prepared garlic, available in jars. Use 5 ml (1 tsp) in place of 1 clove of fresh garlic.

Spicy Chicken Paella

A hot and spicy version of the traditional Spanish dish.

Preparation time: 20 minutes • Cooking time: 40 minutes • Serves: 4

Ingredients

4 chicken legs	1 small cauliflower, broken into florets
2 onions	Salt and freshly ground black pepper
2 cloves garlic	200 g (7 oz) Italian risotto rice
4 tomatoes, skinned	2 sachets ground saffron
2 green or red peppers	10-15 ml (2-3 tsp) chilli powder
60 ml (4 tbsp) sunflower oil	500 ml (18 fl oz) chicken stock

Method

1

Remove the skin from the chicken legs and separate each leg into 2 pieces. Slice the onion and garlic. Remove and discard the hard centres of the tomatoes, roughly chop the flesh and set aside. Seed and dice the peppers and set aside.

2

Heat the oil in a paella pan or large frying pan. Add the chicken pieces and cook until browned all over, turning once.

3

Add the onion and garlic and cook briefly before adding the tomatoes, green or red peppers and cauliflower. Stir to mix, then add seasoning.

4

Scatter the risotto rice into the pan and stir well, add the saffron and chilli powder and stir to mix.

5

Add the chicken stock, stir to mix, then bring to the boil, stirring once or twice.

6

Reduce the heat and simmer, uncovered, for about 30 minutes, or until the chicken and rice are cooked and tender and almost all the liquid is absorbed. Serve immediately.

Serving suggestion

Serve with slices of fresh crusty bread and a mixed leaf and herb salad.

Variations

Use 1-2 spears or heads of broccoli, broken into florets, in place of cauliflower. Use curry powder in place of chilli powder.

Cinnamon Chicken

A tasty chicken casserole, mildly spiced with ground cinnamon and served with tagliatelle.

Preparation time: 20 minutes • Cooking time: 1 hour • Serves: 4-6

Ingredients

1 oven ready chicken, weighing about 1.5 kg (3 lb 5 oz)	250 ml (9 fl oz) white wine
	15 ml (1 tbsp) tomato purée
Salt and freshly ground pepper	250 g (9 oz) celery, finely chopped
100 g (3½ oz) butter	30 ml (2 tbsp) finely chopped fresh parsley
2 red onions, sliced	500 g (1 lb 2 oz) tagliatelle
125 ml (4 fl oz) chicken or vegetable stock	30 ml (2 tbsp) finely grated Parmesan cheese
2 cloves garlic, finely chopped	5-10 ml (1-2 tsp) ground cinnamon
8 tomatoes, skinned and chopped	Fresh parsley sprigs, to garnish

Method

1

Cut the chicken into portions and season with salt and pepper. Melt the butter in a flameproof, ovenproof casserole dish, add the chicken and cook until brown all over. Remove the pan from the heat.

2

Lay the onions over the chicken and cover with stock. Cover and bake in a preheated oven at 200°C/400°F/Gas Mark 6 for 45-60 minutes, or until cooked and tender.

3

Meanwhile, to make the sauce, place the garlic, tomatoes and wine in a saucepan and bring to the boil. Stir in the tomato purée and celery.

4

Season with salt and pepper. Return to the boil, then reduce the heat and simmer for 15 minutes, stirring occasionally. Add the chopped parsley and stir to mix.

5

Meanwhile, cook the pasta in a large saucepan of lightly salted, boiling water for 10-12 minutes, or until al dente. Drain well.

6

Place the pasta on a warmed dish and toss with half the cheese. Spoon the cooked chicken on top of the pasta and sprinkle with cinnamon. Cover with the tomato sauce and sprinkle with grated cheese to serve. Garnish with fresh parsley sprigs and serve immediately.

Serving suggestion

For a substantial meal, serve with oven-baked potatoes or sweet potatoes, cooked green beans and baby sweetcorn.

Variation

Use chopped fresh coriander in place of parsley.

Sweet-and-Sour Chinese Chicken Stir-Fry

A flavourful and colourful quick and easy dish, combining mixed Oriental-style vegetables and tender strips of chicken breast. Add spices and seasonings according to taste.

Preparation time: 15 minutes • Cooking time: 8 minutes • Serves: 2

Ingredients

15 ml (1 tbsp) olive oil	30 ml (2 tbsp) soy sauce
225 g (8 oz) skinless, boneless chicken breast, cut into thin strips or small pieces	30 ml (2 tbsp) tomato ketchup
	15 ml (1 tbsp) honey
1 onion, sliced	1 slice canned pineapple, chopped
1 small red pepper, seeded and sliced	Salt and freshly ground black pepper
1 small green pepper, seeded and sliced	Curry powder, to taste
100 g (3½ oz) canned bean sprouts, drained	Paprika, to taste
75 ml (2½ fl oz) hot vegetable or chicken stock	Cayenne pepper, to taste
	15-30 ml (1-2 tbsp) cornflour
30 ml (2 tbsp) white wine vinegar	30 ml (2 tbsp) chopped fresh chives

Method

1
Heat the oil in a wok or large frying pan. Add the chicken and stir-fry for 2-3 minutes.

2
Add the onion, peppers and bean sprouts and stir-fry for 2-3 minutes.

3
Add the stock, vinegar, soy sauce, tomato ketchup, honey and pineapple and season to taste with salt, pepper, curry powder, paprika and cayenne pepper. Stir-fry for a further 1-2 minutes, or until the chicken and vegetables are cooked and tender.

4
In a small bowl, blend the cornflour with a little water. Add to the wok and stir-fry until thickened and glossy. Adjust the seasoning and serve immediately, sprinkled with chopped fresh chives.

Serving suggestion
Serve with boiled egg or rice noodles

Variations
Use turkey or pork in place of chicken. Use fresh bean sprouts, if available. Use mangetout in place of bean sprouts.

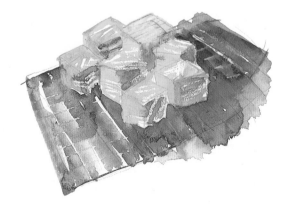

Chicken in Beer

The sauce of this unusual, slightly hot chicken dish is enriched by stout and finished with crème fraîche.

Preparation time: 20 minutes • Cooking time: 40 minutes • Serves: 4

Ingredients

2 small oven-ready chickens, each weighing about 750 g (1 lb 10 oz)	4 tomatoes, skinned and sliced
Salt and freshly ground black pepper	1 sprig of fresh thyme
5-10 ml (1-2 tsp) cayenne pepper	1 bay leaf
3 onions	125 ml (4 fl oz) chicken stock
2 carrots	125 ml (4 fl oz) stout
40 g (1½ oz) butter	125 g (4½ oz) chicken livers, chopped
	30 ml (2 tbsp) crème fraîche

Method

1

Wash the chickens under cold running water, then pat dry with absorbent kitchen paper. Cut each chicken into quarters. Season with salt and pepper and rub cayenne pepper into the skin and flesh. Set aside.

2

Finely chop the onions and coarsely grate the carrots. Set aside.

3

Heat the butter until melted in a large flameproof casserole dish. Add the chicken pieces and cook until browned all over, turning once.

4

Add onions, carrots, tomatoes, thyme and bay leaf, then gradually add the stock, stout and chicken livers and stir to mix.

5

Bring to the boil, cover, reduce the heat and simmer for about 25 minutes, until the chicken is cooked and tender, stirring occasionally. Remove and discard the thyme and bay leaf. Stir in the crème fraîche and reheat gently. Serve hot.

Serving suggestion
Serve with roast potatoes and peas and carrots.

Variations
Use a small can of chopped tomatoes in place of fresh tomatoes. Use cider in place of stout. Use parsnips in place of carrots.

Paprika Chicken

This classic Hungarian dish combines the flavours of paprika and soured cream.

Preparation time: 20 minutes • Cooking time: 40 minutes • Serves: 4

Ingredients

1 chicken, weighing about 1.5 kg (3 lb 5 oz)	30 ml (2 tbsp) ground paprika
Plain flour, to dust	115 g (4 oz) chicken livers, chopped
100 g (3½ oz) streaky bacon	2 beefsteak tomatoes, skinned
1 onion	Salt and freshly ground black pepper
1 clove garlic	250 g (9 oz) soured cream

Method

1

Cut the chicken into 8 pieces, remove and discard the skin and dust with flour. Set aside. Slice the bacon into thin lardons or strips. Finely chop the onion and garlic and set aside.

2

Cook the bacon pieces in a frying pan until the fat becomes glazed. Remove from the pan and set aside on a plate.

3

Add the onion and garlic to the bacon fat and cook until glazed all over, stirring occasionally.

4

Stir in the paprika, cook for 1-2 minutes, then add the chicken pieces to the pan and cover. Cook for about 30 minutes, turning the chicken frequently to cook evenly. After 10 minutes of the cooking time, add the chicken livers and stir to mix.

5

Dice the tomatoes and add to the chicken with the bacon 10 minutes before the end of the cooking time and simmer, uncovered, stirring occasionally.

6

Season to taste with salt and pepper, then fold in the soured cream and reheat gently without boiling before serving.

Serving suggestion

Serve with boiled new potatoes, green cabbage and baby carrots.

Variations

Use smoked bacon for a more complex flavour. Use crème fraîche in place of soured cream.

Cook's tip

Snip bacon into thin lardons or strips using a pair of clean kitchen scissors.

Chicken with Almonds

These lightly spiced chicken legs are baked in a delicious almond crust.

Preparation time: 20 minutes • Cooking time: 45 minutes • Serves: 4

Ingredients

4 chicken legs	5 ml (1 tsp) paprika or hot chilli powder
2 cloves garlic, peeled	A good pinch of cayenne pepper
150 g (5½ oz) ground almonds	45 ml (3 tbsp) butter
2.5 ml (½ tsp) salt	Lemon slices and watercress sprigs, to garnish

Method

1

Remove and discard the skin from the chicken legs and separate the drumsticks from the thighs. Crush the garlic, then rub all over the meat. Set aside.

2

In a bowl, mix the ground almonds with the salt, paprika or chilli powder and cayenne pepper. Set aside.

3

In a saucepan, melt the butter. Remove the pan from the heat. Brush the chicken pieces all over with melted butter, then roll in the almond mixture. Place on a rack in a baking tin.

4

Bake in a preheated oven at 200°C/400F/Gas Mark 6 for about 45 minutes, or until cooked and tender. Serve hot or cold, garnished with lemon slices and watercress sprigs.

Serving suggestion

Serve with oven-baked potatoes and mixed roasted vegetables.

Variations

Use ground cumin or coriander in place of the paprika or hot chilli powder. Use ground hazelnuts in place of almonds.

Chicken in Cognac

Tender chicken breasts are served in a creamy cognac-flavoured sauce for a dinner party treat.

Preparation time: 10 minutes, plus 1 hour marinating time • Cooking time: 50 minutes • Serves: 4-6

Ingredients

800 g (1 lb 12 oz) skinless, boneless chicken breasts	125 ml (4 fl oz) dry white wine
30 ml (2 tbsp) lemon juice	100 g (3½ oz) raisins
Salt and freshly ground black pepper	45 ml (3 tbsp) cognac
100 g (3½ oz) butter	225 g (8 oz) crème fraîche
15 ml (1 tbsp) chopped fresh thyme	Fresh thyme sprigs, to garnish

Method

1

Place the chicken breasts in a shallow, non-metallic dish. Drizzle over the lemon juice and sprinkle with salt and pepper. Cover and set aside in a cool place for 1 hour to marinate.

2

Melt the butter in a large, flameproof casserole dish. Pour in the marinade, then add the chicken and chopped thyme and cook until the chicken is browned all over, turning once or twice.

3

Add the wine and raisins, reduce the heat and simmer for about 30-45 minutes, or until the chicken is cooked and tender, stirring occasionally.

4

In a bowl, stir the cognac into the crème fraîche, then pour over the chicken and heat briefly. Adjust the seasoning and serve hot, garnished with fresh thyme sprigs.

Serving suggestion

Serve with boiled brown or white rice and stir-fried mixed vegetables.

Variations

Use sultanas or chopped ready-to-eat apricots in place of raisins. Use red wine in place of white wine.

Chicken à la Fontaine

A mouth-watering pastry roll filled with a chicken, ham and mushroom mixture – ideal for impressing your guests.

Preparation time: 25 minutes • Cooking time: 40 minutes • Serves: 6

Ingredients

3 skinless, boneless chicken breasts, each weighing about 250 g (9 oz)	*2 tomatoes, skinned and chopped*
Salt and freshly ground black pepper	*250 g (9 oz) cooked mushrooms, thinly sliced*
15 ml (1 tbsp) chopped fresh thyme	*One 300-g (10¹/₂-oz) packet frozen puff or flaky pastry, thawed*
20 g (³/₄ oz) butter	*3 slices ham*
1 onion, finely chopped	*1 egg, beaten, to glaze*
25 g (1 oz) chopped fresh parsley	*Fresh herb sprigs or salad, to garnish*

Method

1

Season the chicken breasts with salt, pepper and thyme. Set aside. Melt the butter in a frying pan, add the chicken and cook until well browned all over, turning occasionally.

2

Remove the chicken from the pan, place on a plate and set aside. Add the onion and parsley to the pan and cook until softened, then add the tomatoes and mushrooms.

3

Cook until the liquid has evaporated, stirring. Season to taste with salt and pepper, then remove the pan from the heat and set aside to cool a little.

4

On a lightly floured surface, roll the pastry out to a rectangle about 30 x 35 cm (approximately 12 x 14 in).

5

Place the ham on the pastry, spread the mushroom mixture over the ham, then place the chicken on top and roll up firmly, pressing the edges together to seal.

6

Brush the pastry with beaten egg and place the roll on a lightly greased baking tray. Bake in a preheated oven at 220°C/425°F/Gas Mark 7 for 20-30 minutes, until cooked, golden and crisp. Serve hot or cold in slices with a fresh herb or salad garnish.

Serving suggestion

Serve with croquette potatoes and cooked broccoli and cauliflower florets.

Variation

Use fresh coriander or basil in place of parsley.

Cook's tip

Roll the pastry out lightly and evenly in one direction only. Always roll away from you, rotating the pastry frequently to retain an even shape. Over-rolled pastry will shrink when baked.

Lime-Roasted Chicken

This unusual dish is refreshing both to the eye and palate, with its delicate green colour and tangy flavour.
Serve as a light main course for a summer dinner party.

Preparation time: 25 minutes, plus 4 hours marinating time • Cooking time: 40 minutes • Serves:4

Ingredients

4 chicken breasts, each weighing about 225 g (8 oz)	*10 ml (2 tsp) white wine vinegar*
Salt and freshly ground black pepper	*75 ml (5 tbsp) olive oil*
	10 ml (2 tsp) fresh chopped basil
4 limes	*Fresh basil sprigs, to garnish*

Method

1
Rub the chicken breasts all over with salt and black pepper. Place in a shallow ovenproof dish and set aside.

2
Using a paring knife or zester, carefully pare away thin strips of rind from 2 of the limes,
then cut these limes in half and squeeze out the juice.

3
In a small bowl, mix together the lime juice and strips of rind, vinegar and 60 ml (4 tbsp) of the oil.

4
Pour the marinade over the chicken breasts. Cover and refrigerate for about 4 hours or overnight.

5
Remove from the refrigerator and baste the chicken thoroughly with the marinade. Place the dish in a preheated
oven at 190°C/375°F/Gas Mark 5 and cook for 30-35 minutes, or until the chicken is well roasted and tender.

6
In the meantime, peel away the rind and pith from the remaining 2 limes. Cut the limes into thin slices using a sharp knife.

7
Heat the remaining oil in a small frying pan and add the lime slices and basil. Cook quickly for 1 minute,
or until the fragrance rises from the basil and the limes just begin to soften.

8
Serve the chicken breasts on a serving platter, garnished with the fried lime slices and sprigs of basil.

Serving suggestion
Serve with baby new potatoes, braised carrots and celery and mangetout.

Variations
Use lemons in place of the limes. Use thyme in place of basil.

Chicken Breasts Stuffed with Mushrooms

In this impressive dish, chicken breasts are stuffed with minced chicken meat, egg and finely chopped mushrooms, then cooked and served with wild mushrooms. The accompanying sauce is made of reduced chicken stock enriched with butter.

Preparation time: 35 minutes • Cooking time: 40 minutes • Serves: 6

Ingredients

225 g (8 oz) button mushrooms	45 ml (3 tbsp) chopped fresh parsley
Juice of ½ lemon	350 g (12 oz) wild mushrooms, such as oyster or shiitake, thinly sliced
115 g (4 oz) butter	
15 ml (1 tbsp) crème fraîche	1 clove garlic
Salt and freshly ground black pepper	350 ml (12 fl oz) chicken stock
7 skinless, boneless chicken breasts	Fresh chervil, to garnish
1 egg, beaten	

Method

1
Cut the button mushrooms into quarters, then place in a food processor with the lemon juice and process until finely chopped. Set aside.

2
Melt 55 g (2 oz) of the butter in a frying pan. When bubbling, add the mushrooms and cook over a high heat for 10 minutes, stirring frequently.

3
Add the crème fraîche, salt and pepper to taste and cook for a further 5 minutes. Remove the pan from the heat and set aside to cool.

4
Process 1 chicken breast in the food processor until minced, then add ½ the beaten egg. Season well. Mix into the cooled mushroom mixture with 15 ml (1 tbsp) of the chopped parsley.

5
Cut open the remaining chicken breasts lengthwise, but do not cut through completely. Season with salt and pepper. Brush the insides of the opened chicken breasts with the remaining beaten egg. Fill each with some of the mushroom stuffing mixture. Close the openings and secure with cocktail sticks, if you like.

6
Cover and steam the stuffed chicken breasts over a pan of boiling water for 15 minutes, or until cooked and tender. Remove the cocktail sticks before serving.

7
Meanwhile, in a frying pan, cook the wild mushrooms in 25 g (1 oz) of the butter over a medium heat. Add 15 ml (1 tbsp) of the parsley, garlic and salt and pepper. Cook for 10 minutes, stirring occasionally.

8
In the meantime, place the stock in a saucepan and boil rapidly to reduce by half. Add the remaining parsley, then gradually mix in the remaining 25 g (1 oz) butter in small pieces using a hand-held electric mixer.

9
Serve the stuffed chicken breasts with the wild mushrooms and the butter sauce spooned over or alongside. Garnish with fresh chervil.

Serving suggestion
Serve with cooked green cabbage or spinach, baby sweetcorn and sautéed potatoes.

Variations
Use fresh coriander or tarragon in place of parsley. Use double cream in place of crème fraîche.

Saffron Chicken Quiche

This luxurious quiche offers an exciting contrast of flavours – rich chicken and warm spices with sharp lemon and parsley rounded off with a sprinkling of sugar. It is ideal for a buffet party.

Preparation time: 25 minutes • Cooking time: 40 minutes • Serves: 4

Ingredients

23-25 x 5 cm (9-10 x 2 in) flan dish, lined with rich shortcrust pastry	350 g (12 oz) chicken meat, cut into long strips
	10 ml (2 tsp) ground cinnamon
8 eggs	2.5 ml (½ tsp) white pepper
55 g (2 oz) butter	15 g (½ oz) fresh parsley, including stalks, coarsely chopped
55 g (2 oz) onion, finely chopped	
90 ml (6 tbsp) lemon juice	5 ml (1 tsp) sugar
3 sachets powdered saffron	Fresh parsley sprigs, to garnish

Method

1

Line the pastry case with greaseproof paper and cover with baking beans. Place in a preheated oven at 200°C/400°F/Gas Mark 6 and bake for 10 minutes. Carefully remove the beans and the greaseproof paper and return the flan to the oven for a further 10 minutes, until the pastry is just cooked.

2

Lightly whisk 1 egg white, reserving the yolk, and brush onto the pastry base.
Return again to the oven for a few minutes, to seal the pastry.

3

In a pan, melt the butter, add the onion, lemon juice and saffron and cook gently until the onion is very soft.

4

Stir in the chicken, cook gently for 5 minutes, then set aside to cool.

5

In a bowl, beat the cinnamon and white pepper into the eggs, then stir in the parsley and cooking juices from the chicken.

6

Arrange the chicken neatly on the cooled pastry case and spoon over the egg mixture.
Cook in a preheated oven at 160°C/325°F/Gas Mark 3 for 15 minutes.

7

Remove the quiche from the oven and sprinkle with sugar, then cook for a further 25 minutes, until lightly browned just around the edges and only just set. Cut into wedges and serve warm or cold, garnished with parsley sprigs.

Serving suggestion

Serve with a selection of salads, such as a mixed leaf salad, coleslaw and a rice salad.

Variations

Use turkey in place of the chicken. Use fresh coriander in place of parsley.

Cook's tip

Do not overcook quiche, otherwise the eggs will toughen. The filling will firm up once the quiche has cooled slightly.

Chicken à la Tante Martine

A wonderfully rich, classic French casserole – ideal to serve at a family get-together.

Preparation time: 25 minutes • Cooking time: 1⅓-1½ hours • Serves: 4

Ingredients

1 oven-ready chicken, weighing about 1 kg (2 lb 4 oz)	*100 ml (3½ oz) fl oz) red wine*
Salt and freshly ground black pepper	*100 ml (3½ fl oz) chicken stock*
15 ml (1 tbsp) vegetable oil	*4 cloves garlic, crushed*
50 g (1¾ oz) bacon, sliced into thin strips	*1 bunch chopped fresh thyme or parsley*
2 onions, sliced	*50 g (1¾ oz) bamboo shoots, chopped*
75 ml (5 tbsp) cognac	*1 bay leaf*
	1 whole clove

Method

1

Wash the chicken under cold running water, cut into pieces and season with salt and pepper.

2

Heat the oil in a large flameproof, ovenproof casserole dish, add the chicken and bacon and cook until the chicken is browned all over, turning once or twice.

3

Add the onion and cognac to the chicken, then ignite the brandy, shaking the dish so that all the chicken pieces are briefly covered in flames.

4

Stir in the wine, stock, garlic, thyme or parsley, bamboo shoots, bay leaf and clove, mixing well.

5

Cover and bake in a preheated oven at 200°C/400°F/Gas Mark 6 for 1¼-1½ hours, or until the chicken is cooked and tender, stirring once or twice. Remove and discard the bay leaf and clove. Serve hot.

Serving suggestion

Serve with croquette potatoes, broccoli florets and carrot sticks.

Variations

Use smoked bacon in place of unsmoked bacon. Use white wine in place of red wine.

Chicken with Asparagus and Mushrooms

An easy-to-create luxury dish of chicken and tender vegetables, served in a creamy sauce.

Preparation time: 15 minutes • Cooking time: 1 hour 15 minutes • Serves: 4

Ingredients

1 oven-ready chicken weighing about 1 kg (2 lb 4 oz)	25 g (1 oz) plain flour
	175 g (6 oz) cooked asparagus
2 leeks, sliced	150 g (5½ oz) cooked mushrooms, sliced
2 carrots, sliced	60 ml (4 tbsp) white wine
2 sticks celery, sliced	15 ml (1 tbsp) lemon juice
1 medium onion, sliced	5 ml (1 tsp) sugar
1 bay leaf	2 egg yolks
1 whole clove	60 ml (4 tbsp) double or single cream
Salt and freshly ground pepper	A dash of Worcestershire sauce
25 g (1 oz) butter	Fresh herb sprigs, to garnish

Method

1

Place the chicken in a large saucepan with the leeks, carrots, celery, onion, bay leaf and clove. Cover with boiling water, add salt and pepper and simmer, covered, for about 1 hour, or until the chicken is cooked and tender.

2

Remove the chicken, place on a plate and set aside. Strain the stock through a sieve, reserving 500 ml (18 fl oz) stock. Discard the vegetables.

3

Remove and discard the skin and bones from the chicken, and slice the larger pieces of chicken. Set aside.

4

Melt the butter in a saucepan, stir in the flour and cook for 1 minute, stirring. Gradually whisk in the reserved stock, then bring to the boil, whisking continuously, until the sauce comes to the boil and thickens. Simmer gently for 2 minutes, stirring.

5

Stir in the chicken and cook for 5 minutes, stirring occasionally.

6

Add the asparagus and mushrooms to the sauce and let them cook briefly. Add the wine, lemon juice and sugar. Lightly blend the egg yolks with the cream and Worcestershire sauce and fold into the sauce. Cook gently, briefly, but do not allow the sauce to boil. Adjust the seasoning and serve immediately, garnished with fresh herb sprigs.

Serving suggestion

Serve with creamed potatoes and a selection cooked baby vegetables such as courgettes and sweetcorn.

Variations

Use wild mushrooms in place of standard mushrooms. Use crème fraîche in place of cream.

Cook's tip

If fresh asparagus is not available, use canned (drained) asparagus in its place.

Braised Chicken with Tarragon

These succulent chicken portions served in a white wine and cream sauce flavoured with tarragon
are ideal served with crispy roast potatoes and seasonal vegetables.

Preparation time: 15 minutes • Cooking time: 1 hour • Serves: 4-6

Ingredients

1 oven-ready chicken, weighing about 1.8 kg (4 lb)	*200 ml (7 fl oz) dry white wine*
	500 ml (18 fl oz) double or single cream
Salt and freshly ground black pepper	*250 g (9 oz) crème fraîche*
55 g (2 oz) butter	*100 g (3½ oz) chopped fresh tarragon*
1 onion, finely chopped	*Fresh herb sprigs, to garnish*

Method

1

Cut the chicken into 8 pieces and rub salt and pepper into the skin and flesh. Set aside.

2

Melt the butter in a frying pan, add the chicken and cook until browned all over, turning once or twice.

3

Add the onion and cook briefly before adding the wine, cream and crème fraîche.

4

Stir in the tarragon and bring to the boil. Cover, reduce the heat and simmer for 45-60 minutes,
until the chicken is cooked and tender, stirring occasionally.

5

Using a slotted spoon, remove the chicken to a plate, cover and keep hot.

6

Bring the sauce in the pan to the boil, then boil rapidly until reduced. Adjust the seasoning.
Serve the hot chicken with the sauce poured over. Garnish with fresh herb sprigs.

Serving suggestion

Serve with duchesse potatoes and broccoli florets.

Variation

Use red onion in place of standard onion.

Chicken in Leek Sauce

A simple yet deliciously rich dish of pan-fried chicken breasts served with a flavourful creamy leek sauce.

Preparation time: 15 minutes • Cooking time: 20-30 minutes • Serves: 4

Ingredients

4 skinless, boneless chicken breasts, each weighing 125-150 g (4^1/$_2$-5^1/$_2$ oz)	30 ml (2 tbsp) Noilly Prat
Salt and freshly ground pepper	250 ml (9 fl oz) white wine
2 leeks	125 ml (4 fl oz) double cream
100 g (3^1/$_2$ oz) butter	125 g (4^1/$_2$ oz) crème fraîche
1 shallot, finely chopped	30 ml (2 tbsp) chopped fresh chives

Method

1
Wash the chicken fillets, pat dry with absorbent kitchen paper and season with salt and pepper. Set aside. Wash and slice the leeks and cook in boiling salted water for 5 minutes, or until cooked and tender. Remove and drain. Set aside and keep warm.

2
Melt the butter in a frying pan, add the chicken and shallot and cook for 15-20 minutes, or until the chicken is cooked, tender and browned all over, turning once or twice. Remove to a plate, cover and keep hot.

3
Add the Noilly Prat, wine, cream and crème fraîche to the pan and cook for a few minutes.
Add the leeks and cook gently for 5 minutes, stirring occasionally.

4
Adjust the seasoning and stir in the chopped chives. Serve the hot chicken with the leek sauce poured over.

Serving suggestion
Serve with mixed brown and wild rice and fresh vegetables such as grilled peppers, courgettes and aubergines.

Variations
Use parsley or tarragon in place of chives. Use another dry vermouth in place of the Noilly Prat.

Cook's tip
To prepare leeks, trim off and discard the root and top and slit down the length of the leeks. Wash thoroughly under cold running water to remove all dirt and grit between the layers. Slice or chop as required.

Index